Exploring the Art of Plotting

THE WRITER'S BOOKSHELF

THE WRITER'S BOOKSHELF

Exploring the Art of Plotting

DiAnn Mills

Bold Vision Books
PO Box 2011
Friendswood, Texas 77549

Copyright © DiAnn Mills 2021
ISBN 978-1-946-708-62-5
Library of Congress Control Number 2021937652

All rights reserved.
Published by Bold Vision Books, PO Box 2011, Friendswood,
Texas 77549 www.boldvisionbooks.com

Published in association with literary agent Janet Grant of Books
and Such Literary Management, www.booksandsuch.com

Cover Art by Amber Weigand-Buckley and Lisa Burns Cover
Design by Barefaced Creative
Interior design by kae Creative Solutions
Published in the United States of America.

Dedication

- Julie Garmon: I appreciate your insight. Thank you, my friend.

- Edie Melson: We are a team!

- Karen Porter: Your encouragement turns my challenges into strengths.

Table of Contents

Introduction

Story is a living, breathing organism. It's fresh, intimate, exciting, and a thrilling accounting of someone's struggle with the pressures of their world to reach a goal or solve a problem.

DiAnn Mills: "Writing - turning straw into gold."

The development takes the wants and needs of humanity and shows us how to experience life from a perspective that may or may not resemble our own. From the beginning of man's existence, we have told stories to offer a snapshot of the meaning of our existence. The steps leading to success or failure, an epiphany or blindness is a walk through plot.

I've read countless books, blogs, and articles on how to plot a novel by master storytellers. Add to that list the many podcasts, workshops, videos, conferences, and panel discussions designed to educate the writer on the many twists and turns of plotting.

In the following pages, the writer will explore the gems I've found that make a plot work: how it's developed, how to overcome obstacles, and how to increase stakes.

I use protagonist, hero or heroine, character, and story player interchangeably. I also use antagonist, opposition, and character interchangeably.

Two other terms I'll use interchangeably: literary tool and technique as applied to the context of our writing.

Dear writer, you will be stretched, pulled, and molded, but the process will enhance your plotting skills. Each chapter ends with exercises, consisting of prompts and questions to help you shape and strengthen an amazing story. Let's get started!

Chapter 1
Reader Expectations

Writers create for their readers' enjoyment. A reader's enthusiasm for story motivates writers to spend hours, days, months, and sometimes years on a novel. But readers are a peculiar species: loving, demanding, critical, finicky, complimentary, and sometimes difficult to please. If they love the story, they will devour every book the author has ever written. They will recommend you to other readers, contact you, and write glowing reviews. If they find dissatisfaction, they will move on to another writer and never return. And why not, when there are millions of novels begging for attention?

The writer's job is to entice the reader to continue the excitement, as though every word of the story is intrinsic to life. No pressure.

The readers of yesterday—fifty, a hundred years or more ago—opened a novel to discover a character's adventure. Today's readers flip open a novel to discover what they will experience on an adventure. The role of a reader is no longer viewed as a spectator, but a participant.

This paradigm for readers changes how writers approach plot. The bar raises to reader experience and a reflection upon the world as the reader perceives. The model chooses emotional involvement and reflects character happenings in the reader's life. We want our readers primarily entertained. That's a writer's number one focus. But we also strive to meet reader-needs by inspiring them to attempt a new task or seek to better their lives physically, mentally, and spiritually. Encouragement that builds self-esteem and confidence in who they are broadens our readers' appreciation of our stories.

While some writers may fault readers as self-centered, I disagree. Through characters overcoming struggles, readers grasp hope for a better tomorrow and meet challenges with clearer insight and wisdom. Can we writers put a price on the time and effort needed to enrich our readers' lives?

Donald Maass writes, "Plot, too, can be understood as a sequence of emotional milestones."

The reader wants to see writer promises and delivery. Accomplish this through a distinct point of view, foreshadowing, increasing stakes, powerful hooks, a red herring, unmet psychological needs, and a host of other literary techniques. No word must be wasted, or the reader rejects the story.

Agenda-driven stories are a disappointment. Let readers form their own opinions about social, political, cultural, or religious issues from watching a character in action.

Note to writer: the reader can spot an agenda driven novel like a bloodhound corners a rabbit.

Novelists have seven feats to accomplish, and all are about satisfying their readers:

1. The reader experiences the story adventure vicariously through a point of view character, usually the protagonist.

2. The reader values a unique protagonist who vows determination and shows the ability to learn and acquire the tools to succeed.

3. The reader admires an unpredictable plot. "Whoa, I didn't see that coming, but it makes sense."

4. The reader sees an antagonist who is a worthy opponent.

5. The reader worries and cares about the protagonist.

6. The character and reader struggle through one conflict after another, each struggle builds from the previous scene.

7. The reader realizes the high stakes from the first chapter.

Every genre has guidelines to meet reader expectations: mystery, suspense, thriller, romance, western, historical, sci-fi, fantasy, and a mix of romance with every genre. Study the guidelines to ensure your story captures the essence of genre and pleases readers.

DiAnn Mills: "If a writer cannot offer hope, what's the purpose of penning another word?"

Explore Deeper

1. What is your genre? Do you understand the guidelines?

2. Write a paragraph about your ideal reader.

3. How do you plan to please your reader?

4. What plotting techniques do you need to enhance your readers' experience?

5. How do you measure up in the seven feats to accomplish in order to please your reader?

Chapter 2
How Does Plot Affect Story?

Plotting is an art, a skillful expression of a writer's creativity and imagination that sends a protagonist on an adventure. It is aesthetic, evocative, and invokes powerful emotions through the actions of three-dimensional characters who strive to achieve a goal.

The character's goal thrives on wanting something so badly that the protagonist or antagonist will venture to any lengths or depths to possess it. A want becomes a need when the character plods ahead to obtain it and nothing exceeds prominence in the character's life but reaching the goal or solving the problem. The characters incorporate sacrifices—physical, mental, and/or spiritual in their quest.

The above explains an arduous but not impossible task. It's a holistic process that fuses scenes and sequels with every novel-writing technique to create a thrilling story.

Integrating skill and various literary techniques begin with one dominant factor—exceptional characterization to carry out the actions of the protagonist and antagonist. Our story players drive our story, which means mastering plot begins with a hero or heroine who yanks on the writer's heart and mind with a problem.

The protagonist accepts the challenge of the hardships and potential victories ahead and secures some skills along the way.

The trek through the carefully crafted pages is called the plot or storyline, and it fills each with unforeseen action which propels the story forward. On the heels of the protagonist is a well-defined antagonist who exceeds the hero/heroine's skills by using cunning, manipulative, charming, or clever means to leave the protagonist in the trenches. The antagonist shows his/her traits by a relentless pursuit that knows no boundaries.

A writer shoves aside a cardboard story player to show a representation of life through the eyes of a distinctive character who brims with lifelike qualities. The characters explode onto the page and propel the story through one exciting scene after another with rising stress, tension, and conflict. The plot builds on each preceding happening to a climax and resolution, resulting in a story that lives in the reader's heart long after the last sentence. But the objective involves the writer weaving dialogue, setting, emotion, exposition, and point of view on a memorable journey.

Through each scene, the protagonist faces challenges that force him/her to change and grow. During this time, the antagonist consistently tosses obstacles in the way. At the climax, the protagonist overcomes an inner flaw to accomplish a physical feat required to possess the story goal.

Plot rises out of the protagonist's strengths and weaknesses, wants and needs, and dreams and desires. Motivation is the fuel behind the protagonist's actions. Unleash the story player onto the page in an adventure according to genre and the established story world. Listen to the protagonist expound his/her needs by watching him/her in action. How a protagonist responds to triumphs and tragedies reveals the real inner self. The truth is evident in every breath.

But desire is not enough for a character's success. A writer establishes the protagonist who has courage, training, education, and stamina to accomplish what appears impossible.

Plot moves forward when the protagonist steps onstage. Conflicts unfold, and character develops through experiencing life, making decisions, and accepting the consequences. These choices should be hard, raw, and sacrificial with an unwavering high risk of failure.

The unpredictable events resulting from the protagonist and antagonist's choices are based on personality, inherited traits, and life experiences. Blend emotions into the mix, especially emotions striving for prominence, and the reader keeps turning pages.

 Ray Bradbury: "Remember plot is no more than footprints left in the snow after your character's have run by on their way to incredible destinations."

Plotting Methods

Plotting methods vary according to the writer's personality and preference. According to the writer's diligence to educate him/herself about the craft, he/she uses a constantly developing process. No matter the chosen method, the writer's tool belt is loaded with a myriad of techniques. The following are the basic plotting methods. One may fit you.

Some novelists carefully outline. They express their artistry through pages of detailed scenes, outlining anywhere from twenty-five to one hundred pages of prewriting information. When they are ready to write their story, they have a completed roadmap.

Some novelists "fly by the seat of their pants" (pantser) writers. Their preference is to discover characters and story each time they sit at the computer. They believe an outline is laborious and would change story content too many times to assemble. A first draft is an exercise in originality. Once the vision of the story has been written, editing begins.

Some novelists choose an organic approach. Studying character and showing a story takes precedence over other means of plotting. Every action and reaction flow from a protagonist to create a harmonious effect that is not only unpredictable but also believable.

Some novelists use a hybrid blend of outlining, pantser, and organic methods. Their brains operate on a mix of knowledge and discovery.

Any of the above methods can and will produce outstanding books. This book is not about teaching you how to outline or persuading you to take the pantser road or a mix. Instead, we will discuss and show mastering the art of plot through sound principles that will provide a foundation for your story.

"To uncover the plot of your story don't ask what should happen but what should go wrong. To uncover the meaning of your story, don't ask what the theme is, but rather, what is discovered. Character making choices to resolve tension—that's your plot. If our protagonist has no goal, makes no choices, has no struggle to overcome, you have no plot." Steven James

Establishing a plot involves studying every aspect of novel writing to map out the best way for a protagonist to reach a goal. The road can be treacherous, and at times forging ahead looks impossible. That's the adventure!

"If you want to write fiction, the best thing you can do is take two aspirins, lie down in a dark room, and wait for the feeling to pass. If the feeling persists, you probably ought to write a novel." Lawrence Block

Explore Deeper

1. What is your definition of plot?

2. Examine the methods of structuring a novel: outliner, pantser, organic, and hybrid. Does your method of plotting fit into one of these categories? Which one?

3. Do you have a credible, 3-dimensional protagonist who has the traits to be a hero or heroine?

4. Does the protagonist established in the above question have the background necessary to move forward? What makes him/her unique to the plot?

5. Do you have a credible, 3-dimensional antagonist who has the traits to overcome a hero or heroine?

6. What traits or skills ensure the antagonist is worthy opposition?

7. Establish your protagonist's problem or goal.

8. What is stopping the protagonist from achieving the goal?

9. Establish the antagonist's problem or goal?

10. What is stopping the antagonist from achieving the goal?

Examine the scenario below. Choose one of the character scenarios to write the scene.

A man is hurrying to his car. He's late leaving the office and late to see his son play soccer. Someone jerks on his arm. He's swung around and faces two teenage boys who are attempting to snatch his wallet.

The man is:

☐ Off duty cop

☐ A lawyer

☐ A pastor

☐ In the middle of a panic attack

What traits would a hero or heroine need to accomplish the scenario below?

My childhood memories of the beauty of eastern Kentucky played before my eyes. Autumn had wrapped its cloak around the hills, bathing them in scarlet and gold. I smelled the crispness in the air and the promise of a chilly night by the fireplace. I longed to gather apples, nuts, and root vegetables with no worries for tomorrow. Here I'd find healing—here where no one knew me or my sordid past.

Chapter 3
Story basics:
Theme, Idea, Concept, Premise

This chapter clarifies a few definitions that sometimes confuse the writer about plotting. Before moving forward on your story project, take the time to familiarize yourself with the terms.

DiAnn Mills: "Learning the craft of writing, like any skill, is a lifelong experience. Embrace it. Crave it. Treasure it."

Theme

Theme is the psychological message a story conveys, the truth or meaning behind the story, the subtle fuel that leads the writer to create and what many readers grasp at the end. Writers determine theme by showing the protagonist's internal problem that must be overcome before he/she can reach the goal. The theme becomes the motivating factor resulting in conflict, which we'll discuss in a future chapter.

Theme Ideas:

- ☐ Love and hate
- ☐ Good vs evil
- ☐ Guilt
- ☐ Forgiveness
- ☐ Justice
- ☐ Prejudice
- ☐ Survival
- ☐ Rich vs poor
- ☐ Identity or coming of age
- ☐ Power
- ☐ And many more

Story Idea

A story idea is like trekking into an unexplored wilderness. The hike is rough, dangerous, and filled with obstacles. Sometimes we question our sanity and the value of spending hours venturing toward an exciting destination.

A writer's idea is valuable, but what does a writer do with something that exists only in the mind? The mental image attracts us, lures us to consider an incredible story, and we long to move forward. But how? Not every idea will emerge into a powerful story unless the writer applies specific criteria to take the idea to the next creative level.

Ideas are everywhere. All we need do is look around us. Every breath is someone's story, a gem to develop from a writer's unique perspective. Oh, the possibilities to generate our next novel:

- ☐ Devotions
- ☐ Dreams
- ☐ Fears
- ☐ Scripts
- ☐ Blog posts
- ☐ Movies

- [ ] Nightmares
- [ ] TV shows
- [ ] Memories
- [ ] Poetry
- [ ] Conversations
- [ ] Nonfiction books
- [ ] Documentaries
- [ ] Genealogy
- [ ] Media headlines
- [ ] Family history
- [ ] Magazine articles
- [ ] And the list goes on.

Observe people and situations in different settings for additional ideas. This aspect of story writing can't be learned in a book. Seeing others in action stirs our artistic expression. My favorite areas are malls, zoos, airports, restaurants, and recreational spots.

According to Christopher Booker in *The Seven Basic Plots: Why We Tell Stories*, all storylines fall into seven plot types. These basic archetypes are:

1. Overcoming the Monster
2. Rags to Riches

3. The Quest

4. Voyage and Return

5. Comedy

6. Tragedy

7. Rebirth

While all the plots have been written and our books can slide into one of these categories, a story idea takes its originality from the writer's personality, values, imagination, and life experiences. Much like a well-developed character looks at the world from a distinct point of view, a story takes life from the one who fashions it.

A writer takes an idea and moves forward with a concept, much like peeling back the layers of an onion.

Orson Scott: "Everybody walks past a thousand story ideas every day. The good writers are the ones who see five or six of them. Most people don't see any."

Concept

A concept is the foundation of our story. Alone, the statement means nothing, but the writer uses concept to build a premise.

Larry Brooks: "A concept is a central idea or notion that creates context for a story."

Premise

How does a writer take a raw concept and shape it into a polished premise?

Larry Brooks: "Premise is NOT concept. But it can be fueled by whatever is conceptual about the story (stated separately within a pitch as the story's concept). Premise is the summarized description of a story. And when that story is considered fresh and powerful, premise emerges from a conceptual landscape."

Idea example: A young woman learns a terrible truth about her grandfather.

Concept example: A young woman idolizes her grandfather, who raised her until they are torn apart by tragedy.

What can a writer do with that example?

Premise example:

> A young woman idolizes her grandfather who raised her, a man who owns a large concrete construction business that specializes in bridge construction. She discovers a discrepancy in his business practices and searches for him to clarify what she's found. She witnesses him murder a man, an employee who learned the grandfather is taking construction shortcuts that weaken bridges. The young woman searches her grandfather's computer and discovers more than she ever imagined. He walks in on her and threatens her if she tells anyone.

Should the writer settle for the first premise that enters her mind? Not if she wants a story that exceeds an agent, editor, or reader's expectations.

With a strong premise, a writer examines the many possibilities that can arise from one sentence. Several what-ifs play into the storyline. Let's take another look at our premise. What is the worst possible scenario that can happen?

1. The young woman's grandfather learns she witnessed the murder. He confronts her to convince her the killing was in self-defense.

2. The young woman's grandfather learns she witnessed the murder. He threatens to blame her if she tells anyone.

3. The young woman's grandfather learns she witnessed the murder. He has too much money invested in his operation to allow his granddaughter to stand in his way. He must eliminate her.

4. The young woman disappears. She changes her identity and lives in fear until she meets a man who detects she is hiding from something evil.

5. The young woman flees to local law enforcement officers who don't believe her.

6. The young woman didn't see the murder, only the smoking gun. But she believes her grandfather committed the killing.

Continue with the worst scenario until the writer can develop an unexpected yet believable premise.

I suggest using the established premise to show how the antagonist will overcome the protagonist. This is an even worse-possible scenario because it gives the antagonist a concrete footing into taking over the goal.

Brainstorming with another writer(s) frees up our minds to think beyond our self-imposed box. They see our story as a game; we see the story as our protagonist's race against time and the atrocious work of the antagonist.

A story theme may or may not form at the idea stage, but by the end of the story, theme rises like rich cream. An idea merges into a concept, and a concept merges into a well-developed premise. No matter the writer's method of creating the story, the proof of the writer's skill is in the finished project.

Explore Deeper

1. What is your story's theme?

2. What is your story idea?

3. What is your concept?

4. What is your premise?

5. What are at least three exciting scenarios in which to develop your premise?

6. Write a paragraph about your story as you see it now. Not an outline, because not all of us plot the same way. This is a story idea. The art of creating story means the writer can change anything as often as necessary to show only your protagonist could have made the impossible journey.

7. Repeat the criteria in numbers 1 through 6 and apply the content to your antagonist.

8. Are there specific scenes that roll around in your head, the must-haves in the story? Write them down. These don't need to be chronological at this point.

Chapter 4
The High Concept Novel

Every writer longs to hear her story premise is a high concept novel. Agents and editors battle to secure that coveted, marketable, reader-captivating story; although stats say roughly 5 percent of submissions meeting that criteria fall into the high concept category. The irony is defining a high concept novel differs according to who's answering the question.

In Chapter 3, we discussed a theme, idea, concept, and premise. Each one adds to the development of the story. But in a high concept novel, the premise becomes the pitch and drives the story forward. It clearly relays an easily understood story idea, genre, originality, and distinctive qualities in approximately 3 minutes.

Perhaps the story has strong movie potential. The plot doesn't have to be new, but the spin or twist must be unprecedented.

Writer, if the plot line of your story is complicated or the pitch takes longer than three sentences, it's not a high concept. Publishers release low concept stories—lots of them in every genre. But if we are seeking high concept status for our stories, we need to look at the following guidelines:

- ☐ The short premise steps beyond unique, distinct, and amazing to unparalleled. Each word packs a punch, increasing the desire for more of the adventure.

- ☐ The protagonist hits the top of the likability chart.

- ☐ The story appeals to a wide audience. Readers create a buzz that translates into book sales. No matter the genre, readers flock to read the story.

- ☐ The external and internal conflict applies to many readers. They identify with the struggles and more easily envision the adventure.

- ☐ The characters' emotions play a critical role and easily engage the reader.

☐ The plot often takes something ordinary and adds an ingenious/clever slant or twist that isn't easily answered.

☐ The goal for the protagonist looks unattainable.

☐ The novel is well written. Period.

Not all the above have to be in place for a high concept novel, but the more traits increase the likelihood.

For the writer, a risk enters the equation because he/she must deliver a power-packed novel that exceeds reader expectations. Many writers say this is true for all novels, and they are right. Successful writers take the common and mine all the possibilities with incredible vision and insight. Study these high concept ideas that became books and movies. Note, I've included a sample of genres, not an exhaustive list. Many others came to mind. I encourage you to read these books and watch the movies to dissect how and why these flew to the top of the bestseller and top movie lists.

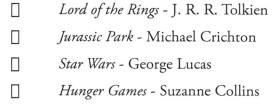

☐   *Lord of the Rings* - J. R. R. Tolkien

☐   *Jurassic Park* - Michael Crichton

☐   *Star Wars* - George Lucas

☐   *Hunger Games* - Suzanne Collins

☐　*The Da Vinci Code* - Dan Brown

☐　*Life of Pi* - Yann Martel

☐　*Harry Potter* - J. K. Rowling

☐　*The Chronicles of Narnia* - C. S. Lewis

Where does a writer find the idea and concept that meets the specifications for a high concept novel? Are you willing to explore the following?

1. Expand your mind by getting alone. Turn off the noise and leave technology behind. Where do your thoughts take you?

2. Research Greek, Roman, and Celtic mythology. Can you take one of those story worlds and create a contemporary novel?

3. Visualize your novel as a film. Will it easily translate to the screen?

4. Explore scientific phenomena. Is there an incident or discovery that piques your interest?

5. How can you make the seemingly impossible credible?

6. Read a chapter in Proverbs. Now flip the life lesson.

7. Spend time with children. Free your imagination to mirror their minds and creativity.

8. What if everything you believe as truth is a lie? How could you expose it in a manner that is believable?

9. What personality types irritate you? How could you learn to like a person with those traits?

10. Create a new race of people. What are their values, appearance, culture, homes, jobs, etc., that is radically different from yours?

11. Rewrite the ending of a fairy tale. How would you change the plot?

12. What disturbs you? What would it take for that incident/happening to affect you positively?

13. This is perhaps the hardest ... What is an original idea?

Not every novel idea will be termed high concept as a sought-after read, but a wise writer seeks to design a story that resonates with a wide audience.

Explore Deeper

1. Examine your current story premise. Is it a high concept novel? Why or why not?

2. How can you brainstorm your premise to increase marketability?

3. Research your new concept. Does the story line sound familiar?

4. How does your new idea affect the characters?

5. How does your new idea affect the reader?

6. Are you pleased with the results?

Plot the storyline below:

What if Snow White aligned herself with the dark side?

Princess Snow White tricks her kind-hearted parents into eating poison apples so she can take over the throne. But a prince sees through her treachery and raises up an army of dwarfs to overthrow her.

Chapter 5
The Power of Setting

Ah, setting, the frail stepchild of fiction. How often we neglect this vital component of story, by declaring it unimportant when setting is more than a backstage player or a minor role. We dress her in rags, have her clean the chimney, then criticize her for lack of muscle. We forget setting can be the glass slipper ushering a plot into a bestselling novel.

Setting is the physical environment where a story takes place. A strong setting challenges character, plot, dialogue, and narrative by adding a twist in the protagonist's journey to reach a goal. True setting makes the goal harder to obtain, an often unforeseen means of driving plot.

Explore the power of where a scene takes place and note how a unique setting takes skill. But once mastered, it gives the story an extra dimension by adding stumbling blocks for the protagonist in every scene.

Establish the time, date, season, and culture of where the story takes place. How does the setting affect the character psychologically? Show enough setting for readers to envision the story world—and no more. Remember, our readers must experience the story from their perspective.

Use sensory perception to root the protagonist into her surroundings. Sights, smells, sounds, tastes, and touch paint the scene. If the writer tells too much, readers will skip the description and move on to the action, and they might miss an important detail. In addition, information overload cheats readers of vicariously living the adventure and closes the door on imagination.

The more credible a writer shapes the setting, the more he/she adds strength to a story because it forces the character to respond.

A character who lives in the setting will not make the same observations as a visitor who will most likely make a few mistakes to survive. For example, a veteran police officer comprehends the demands and unpredictable nature of his job better than a rookie who exhibits nervous or overconfident traits.

Note the emotions that differentiate a seasoned character from a novice in a specific environment. The seven universal emotions, according to Tonya Reiman in The Power of Body Language, are surprise, fear, anger, sadness, disgust, happiness, and contempt. Move your characters around in the setting and initiate a psychological response. Use active verbs and powerful nouns to show more about the real inner story player.

A writer chooses at least one of the following scenarios to create a story setting with visceral impact:

- [ ] Man vs. man
- [ ] Man vs. animal
- [ ] Man vs. nature
- [ ] Man vs. society
- [ ] Man vs. survival
- [ ] Man vs. technology
- [ ] Man vs. God

An unexpected change in a protagonist's environment reveals the true inner self by displaying strength or weakness. Does the protagonist run or stand and fight? Sometimes fleeing translates as courage. The adversity can be obvious or hidden but include the deception in ways that force the story player to make tough decisions. Always challenge the protagonist to step out from their comfort zone.

Antagonistic Setting

Using setting as an antagonist increases stress, tension, and conflict for the protagonist striving to achieve a goal. To ensure a tight, high-stakes scene, use the character's fears and weaknesses against him/her. Every scene requires a setting, a distinct situation in which the writer can harvest the gems of antagonism.

Assign traits that defy the protagonist's goals and raise the stakes. Stop the character from moving forward by establishing a barrier that ensures temporary defeat.

This forces the character not only to struggle but also to face an inner and outer antagonist: fear and setting. Fear will be discussed more in Chapter 7. Outline the characteristics of an unexpected force rising against the protagonist—and watch plot twists emerge that can take the story deeper.

Setting is vital and full of spirit, but an antagonistic setting means shaky ground for the protagonist. Survival extends beyond defeating a villain, either physical, mental, or spiritual. Every breath equates to potential disaster.

An antagonistic setting gives a plot power.

An antagonistic setting is as much a gift to the reader as an intricate story line.

Physical

Usually setting is physical, as in an unexpected storm, rough terrain foreign to the protagonist, a natural disaster, a work or home environment that is explosive or a geographic stage that turns hostile.

Mental

An antagonistic setting can be mental as in a dream world, an unconscious state, a hallucination, or altered thinking.

Spiritual

Root spiritual opposition in a belief system that is contrary to truth or the laws of a government or culture ruling the country.

Whatever the location, setting can keep our characters—and the plot—moving in directions that aren't always predictable to the reader. When a surprise occurs, it should be seamless.

View the setting's description as though it were a characterization sketch. Concentrate on a villain's traits: determined, powerful, an outward appearance of beauty or charm, and the ability to manipulate and deceive. Use those traits to disguise what looks like a pleasant environment.

This technique also provides opportunities for strong symbolism. An encroaching forest fire can transform a fabulous vacation home into a death trap. Working for a prestigious company can become a source of evil, as in John Grisham's *The Firm.*

The following are examples of an antagonistic setting in a few popular genres.

Contemporary

A winter retreat at a mountain resort and an opportunity for a man to evaluate his life priorities turns into a struggle for survival when an avalanche traps fifty people inside the resort.

Fantasy

Create a land where all creatures coexist with humans in friendship and love until a dragon king eliminates all those who refuse to pay heavy taxes.

Historical

A wagon train pulls into a peaceful valley where the wagon master assures the weary travelers can find rest and water. But the water is poison, and unrest turns the group against each other in a bloody confrontation.

Romance

A couple honeymoons on an exotic, deserted island. The white, sandy beaches and the call of seagulls resemble a paradise. An unexpected storm rises, bringing high winds and twenty-foot waves. The couple discover they are trapped with no means to contact the outside world for help.

Sci-Fi

An isolated, peaceful planet faces invasion by super-intelligent aliens who require the inhabitants' water supply for their own survival.

Suspense

A woman who believes she has the perfect marriage discovers her husband is smuggling guns to a cartel. She confronts him, and he threatens to kill her.

Thriller

A businesswoman known nationwide for her generosity and outstanding work benefits arranges for her employees to take advantage of in-house medical care, which is a cover for testing potential life-threatening drugs.

Character growth can occur in any setting, whether the environment is expected or unexpected. But the story line doesn't advance by placing the protagonist in idyllic surroundings that make overcoming emotional and physical obstacles easy and pain free. Muddy the waters and create an antagonistic environment.

I hope you now see the power of setting for your story. Study bestselling writers to see how they make settings pivotal. Use your imagination, research, characterization, plot, and genre to create a variety of settings to make your story excel above the others.

Explore Deeper

1. List your protagonist's fears and weaknesses.

2. Now incorporate the items in #1 into various settings that follow your storyline. List those settings below.

3. How do the above settings appeal to the protagonist?

4. How do those settings act against the protagonist?

5. Are any of these settings in unfamiliar territory?

6. How do those settings force the protagonist to deal with his/shortcomings?

7. Look at your current story. How can you incorporate an antagonistic setting?

Chapter 6
Research Tips

Anovelist who explores research, explores life—and life is a story. Research forms the core of a story's credibility. Writers create authentic plot points and develop a story that is true to the setting, time, era, and worldview.

How far will a writer go to ensure the story is factual? What steps will the writer take to ensure the manuscript soars with authenticity? Is the writer ready to step outside the boundaries of his/her comfort zone? This often means traveling to the setting and investigating where the character journeyed on the way to achieving a goal. Only when a writer prepares to conduct research beyond the minimum will readers find reason to applaud.

I've traveled to South Sudan, rode along with the Border Patrol, interviewed serious treasure hunters, became involved with the FBI and their Citizens Academy, the ATF Citizens Academy, and I'm constantly investigating fresh ways to ensure my novel's contents are accurate.

Sensory Perception

Authentic fact-finding enlists sensory perception, and the results draw readers into our story world. Consider not only what a character would see and hear but also what he/she would taste, smell, touch, and sense intuitively. During a research visit, take lots of notes and photos. Bring along a recording device for interviews with people who live there.

See

What the writer sees while conducting research takes many facets or dimensions. Seeing in a physical sense means documenting all those details the writer deems necessary about the story world—yet knowing only one or two items will be necessary. The dialogue, description, and inner thoughts add flavor to the story.

But sight exceeds the physical realm. Consider what's in the mind's eye. A writer's imagination weaves what she sees with how she will use the information.

Logic is another part of seeing the setting. Will the information gathered build realism and story credibility? What have you discovered that brings fresh vision to your character's adventure?

Another aspect of seeing in research is the careful study of the people interviewed. What does their body language reveal as they relay memories? Painful moments? Heart treasures? People remember events according to their own sensory experience. These memories can add a personal touch or help us sort out truth and logic.

Hear

What does the writer hear when conducting research? Listen to the sounds of nature. Study the culture, the unique vocabulary, the subtleties, the laughter, and tears. Writers tune their ears to the dialect of the people within their setting. Several years ago, my son and I visited Gettysburg, PA. We were so moved we thought we heard the cries of the soldiers.

Taste

Communicate local flavor by evoking the sense of taste. Whether we are in the States or halfway around the world, depicting food and drink brings a richness to our writing. Ever watch a travel show? By showing a restaurant, a food vendor, or a meal in someone's home, we offer awareness into that culture. The character's experience with unusual tastes can also evoke fear and confusion.

Smell

Dig into the traditions and customs for the setting's smell, whether offensive or enjoyable. The sense of taste and smell weave memories for us and our characters. The link often means the two are inseparable.

Touch

Researching through touch means brushing our fingers across the vegetation, dipping our feet into the water, petting an animal, or embracing someone or something different. Experience the surroundings. Pick up a baby or hold a hand. Laugh. Cry. Touch pulls us into someone else's world. This may be difficult, but it always brings a reward.

A writer who visits her setting has the advantage of sensory perception while walking the same earth as the character. Obtaining and deciding where to use detail means hard work, but the rewards pay off with more readers. The payoff provides the reader a deeper adventure. I challenge you to lace up your boots and step into an unfamiliar world.

If a writer uses an actual place to set a story, be sensitive to those living in the community. Consider using fictitious names for cities, streets, and businesses to avoid offending the residents. A writer wouldn't want a serial murder living on a real street or cite damaging information about prominent people and places.

A writer needs three essentials to ensure research success:

1. A positive attitude.

2. A temporary personality from an introvert to an extrovert.

3. A list of prepared questions that demand answers.

Sometimes it's impossible for the writer to visit a story's setting. Libraries hold a wealth of information. Websites offer incredible insight, but make sure you verify sources for your online research in at least three places before documenting it in your story. Pick up the phone and call the area. The chamber of commerce often has more information on a subject than any website. Churches, diners, museums, libraries, newspapers, and historical societies are rich sources of information.

Sci-fi and fantasy settings are best researched by reading a myriad of bestselling novels in that genre. Familiarize yourself with ancient myths, folklore, futuristic technology, and preparing a story world.

Research can be a terrifying process or an enjoyable journey simplified by a few helpful tips. How do we conduct the process effectively and efficiently?

Organize

List what the story needs according to a timeline. This includes setting, characters, dialogue, and culture.

Develop

What specialty people does the writer need to contact to ensure reliable information?

Map

Where does the writer need to visit for accuracy and sensory perception?

Focus

The following questions and suggestions will help the writer focus, develop, and map out a strategic plan.

1. Visit the area's Chamber of Commerce.

2. Conduct a google search of the community or area.

3. Take lots of pictures and label them.

4. Interview the local people. In a historical, this also means reading diaries and journals.

5. How has history affected the community?

6. Listen to how the local people talk. Do they have a unique vocabulary?

7. What is the area's culture? What are their values and expectations?

8. What is their diet? How do they obtain their food supply?

9. How is the area governed?

10. What is unique about the restaurants and hotels?

11. What is the source of entertainment?

12. How do residents celebrate the seasons? What are the average temperatures?

13. What are the medical concerns? Is medical care available?

14. Where do the people live? How are their homes constructed?

15. Where do the people shop?

16. How do the people dress?

17. Do the arts play a role in the community?

18. If the area is near a national or state park, look for research material in the visitor center.

19. Know the wildlife and birds of the area.

20. How do the people view education, sports teams, and favorite colleges and universities?

21. How do the people earn a living?

22. Locate a map of the area. Both contemporary and historical maps may aid in backstory development.

23. Visit the local library. Examine newspaper archives.

24. View documentaries.

A note of caution. Research is not about the writer's display of knowledge, but an opportunity for readers to experience the story through the eyes of characters who live and walk the adventure. Use only the information the character needs and in his/her point of view.

True research into our story means an investment to benefit others. Our readers deserve an unforgettable adventure. Ensure the story includes sufficient details to touch hearts and lives. I hope your mind is spinning with possibilities of how to make research play an active role in your story and have fun in the process.

Explore Deeper

1. Have you fully explored every detail of your book's setting?

2. Are you able to visit your setting?

3. What does the character(s) see in your setting?

4. What can the character(s) hear that is unique in your setting?

5. What specific tastes are linked to your setting?

6. What smells does the character(s) associate with the setting?

7. What can the character(s) touch in only your setting?

8. What are the ways your setting can be exceptional?

9. Is online research an asset for you? How?

Chapter 7
Adding a Layer of Fear

Fear doesn't have to make sense to the character; it's present and dangerous. The emotion is not necessarily negative, but an intuitive means of protecting the character from threat of harm. Those threats can be physical, emotional, spiritual, or psychological, and the resulting sensations alert the character to possible danger.

Whether a fear is genuine or imagined, the emotion affects character and requires coping skills. The anxiety and pressure can trap a character, causing him/her to do whatever is necessary to avoid the triggered reaction and response. According to the character's personality, backstory, culture, education, upbringing, and a host of other events make each fear unique. The character can feel alone and ashamed or hide from others to avoid ridicule. To the sufferer, the presumed danger is real. Fear manifests itself in paralysis, shock, seeking safety, fleeing, and/or fighting.

Respecting the outcome of a specific fear doesn't make a hero or heroine any less a person. The character who respects healthy fears shows wisdom in avoiding—running into a burning building, playing golf in an electrical storm, handling a loaded gun, swimming in shark-infested water, and the list goes on. Motivation fuels the choice to fight or flee. Sometimes it takes more courage to run from a harmful situation than to stay and fight.

A phobia is a type of fear that is abnormal and irrational. But to the character, the obsessive behavior that accompanies it is real.

The downside of catering to a phobia:

- ☐ Paranoia
- ☐ Insomnia
- ☐ Deteriorating health
- ☐ Inability to function mentally or physically
- ☐ Destroyed personal and interpersonal relationships.

The reader who experiences the same type of fear will stay engaged in the story. The horror draws the reader closer to the beloved character, and together they walk through a personal nightmare.

Readers long to see their beloved protagonist become a better person, but the fear must be processed logically, and the outcome used as a strength in the climax. The character who survives and learns from facing down an emotional handicap is a role model. The tough who stand to analyze a situation and take healthy steps to move forward, requires a character who values growth and change. He accepts his unhealthy behavior, and his actions coincide with his personality and determination.

The antagonist can use the fear against the protagonist, allowing the writer to weave a stronger plot. And this character has fears, too. Sometimes these unwanted emotions contribute to his/her motive to commit a crime, something unethical, and/or immoral. A protagonist who discovers an antagonist's fears discovers ways to trap the character and end the injustice.

A strong character analyzes the potential fear:

- ☐ How powerful is the danger?
- ☐ Is the danger immediate or in my future?
- ☐ How do I respond to the fear?

A strong character learns from the experience to help others:

- [ ] By empathizing and sympathizing with the emotion.
- [ ] By identifying body language, voice inflections, and behaviors that show fear.
- [ ] By offering coping tools to help others

The merit of using fear in our stories, no matter what genre, adds to the character's arc while pushing ahead in the plot with stress, tension, and conflict. The emotion weaves inner and outer conflict to overcome before the protagonist can achieve a goal. This causes the plot to thicken and adds another layer to the barriers attempting to stop the protagonist. Use any context of fear to confuse the character and create anxiety. Establish plot points that make the character keenly aware of the fear. Intensify it. Culture and social standards also cultivate fear. What resonates in the character's mind because of the emotionally stunned moment? That's what readers remember.

Common writing advice is to write what we know. This includes the heart-pounding, palm-sweating reality of walking through real fears. By creating scenes from personal encounters, the writer transfers credible emotions to the character and thus the reader. Within the writer's transparency dwells realistic behavior.

Fear is a powerful emotion in our lives and our characters. The sensation is undeniable. Strive to understand the reality of the emotion according to your carefully crafted character.

Explore Deeper

1. What terrifies you?

2. What terrifies your character?

3. Is the fear real or a phobia?

4. What is your character's reaction to that fear?

5. Take a few minutes to detail the first time the character encountered the fear. Include who, what, where, when, and if you know ... why.

6. Is the fear appropriate?

7. Does the character want to overcome the emotional paralysis? How will he/she accomplish it?

8. Does the character need help—professional, spiritual, or guidance from a friend or family member?

9. Can overcoming the fear restore the character's self-confidence and move the story forward?

10. Read your answers above. Now write a scene in which your protagonist must face that fear to reach his/her goal.

Chapter 8
Foreshadowing

Foreshadowing is an ingenious literary tool that indicates something will happen in the story. It hints or suggests what is to come and becomes a promise to the reader, a promise that must be kept. Like a road sign that shows what is ahead, foreshadowing signals tension and suspense while alluding to a fear, threat, humor, tragedy, or a specific event—which can be good or bad. The best foreshadow uses subtlety and can mislead the character and reader. It doesn't have to make sense at the time or point to the future.

Foreshadowing falls into one of two categories.

1. **Direct:** The writer purposely wants the reader to know what will happen in order to better reveal the

story happenings. Place this foreshadow in the prologue or first chapter.

2. **Indirect:** The writer alludes to what will happen, and the reader may not be aware of the foreshadowing until it actually occurs.

Writers use various techniques to weave foreshadowing into their stories.

Dialogue

Dialogue offers an opportunity to hint of things to come.

☐ "I've told you repeatedly to stop hanging out with those kids."

☐ "Aw, Mom. You're a teacher. Bill's dad's a cop, and Chad's mom is a judge. How could we get into trouble with parents like that?"

☐ "For once, I wish you'd stick up for yourself."

Thoughts are a more obvious place to foreshadow. Rephrase the dialogue above to show how inner thoughts are more promising because the character is reflecting upon wants, needs, desires, and goals.

☐ Mom had told me repeatedly to stop hanging out with my friends, but she didn't really know them.

☐ Our parents were in law enforcement and understood exactly what we might plan, but we thought about it.

☐ My wife thinks I never stand up for myself.

Symbols use a tangible item to represent something intangible that has a psychological meaning: weather, color, numbers, seasons, various settings, wildlife, memories, hours of the day, and many more. The imagery of the symbol resonates with the character and the reader.

☐ Winter with its bleak white came early and stayed long past its welcome, much like an unwanted guest.

☐ I pulled into my driveway, and a black cat walked in front of my car. It stopped and stared at me as if the feline dared me to move one inch ahead.

☐ She paid for the necklace with the stolen credit card: $666.00.

Emotions

Emotions pack a powerful punch to show how a character reacts and responds to the surrounding happenings. We've talked in previous chapters about the seven universal emotions: surprise, fear, anger, sadness, disgust, happiness, and contempt. Foreshadowing that reaches into the well of a character's emotion strengthens what is to come.

☐ Since she was a little girl, she'd climbed the treacherous cliffs rising from the ocean just to see where the horizon met the water. Only those moments took away the loneliness.

☐ Papa always kept a loaded gun in his nightstand. Not even Mama could touch it.

☐ The ragged little boy hugged me, but his body odor stopped me from returning any affection.

Expectations for the future show a character's inner motivation to achieve a goal. In addition, the direct or indirect foreshadow provides another layer to the plot.

☐ He looked forward to a two-week summer vacation with nothing tasking him but when and where to fish.

☐ I planned my life according to logic: finish my masters, begin a career, then look for a husband whose values matched mine.

☐ Nothing would stop him from earning a law degree. A prestigious law school had accepted him, and he'd secured the funds to pay for it.

In creating a foreshadow, examine the plot and decide where and when the mention should occur. For the outliner, the placement of the technique occurs in the planning stage. For the pantser, the technique's value may surface after the completion of the first draft.

Other categories such as prophecy, culture, and genre incorporate foreshadowing to enhance the storyline and deepen characterization. Readers may or may not comprehend the technique, and that's okay. When readers recognize it, they are even more involved in the adventure. The writer has provided a narrow path for the character and the reader to follow.

Explore Deeper

1. Have you used foreshadowing in your story?

2. In your story opening, create a direct foreshadow that mirrors the character's inner problem.

3. What is an indirect foreshadow you can use in your story?

4. Develop a storyline that uses a prophecy.

5. Is this a direct or indirect foreshadow?

A fifteen-year-old girl enters a new school. As she walks down the hall in search of a classroom, three girls point at her and laugh. Write the plot point that this foreshadows.

Chapter 9
Story Pacing

Story pacing is the writer's ability to move the story ahead with intriguing words and sentence length. The process incorporates the genre, plot, characters, and goal of each scene. Writers strive for varied story structure that balances the mood and emotion with actions and reactions. The technique opens the door to achieving the perfect speed for a story scene. No writer wants the rhythm of their sentences, paragraphs, and scenes to resemble an unchanging metronome or ticking clock.

For the writer who outlines and structures her novel before the actual writing begins, pacing is a part of the intricate process. The pantser prefers a discovery method; a character steps into action and increases the pace and slows during internal reflection. Or the writer uses a mix. As in every technique of novel writing, the story's appeal to readers is the mark of success.

Genre explores pacing to lead the reader into story swells and dips that balance the story. The genre often determines the pace. Horror, suspense, thrillers, and mystery achieve the desired effect by keeping the plot moving ahead in genre-related surges and the threat of impending danger.

Faster pacing ensues action and uses the scene's mood to add stress, tension, and suspense. The variance keeps readers engaged. Their heart rate increases, adding additional emotion to the experience. The speed tells the reader that something exciting is about to happen. Hold on tight! It's coming!

The following tips will help accomplish a faster story pace:

- ☐ Choose an active voice with strong verbs.

- ☐ Create shorter sentences, paragraphs, and scenes. Sometimes a one-word sentence says more than a paragraph.

- ☐ Develop action driven hooks at the beginning and ending of a scene.

☐ Enlist snappy dialogue.

☐ Focus on shorter words and hard consonant sounds.

☐ Hold back on reaction scenes.

☐ Incorporate figurative speech that indicates time critical to the scene. For example: a ticking clock, waves crashing against the shore, or a dripping faucet. Thus the symbol also adds emotional depth.

☐ Limit characters in a scene.

☐ Narrow the plot.

☐ Raise the stakes in the scene/chapter hooks.

A slower pace calms readers. They relax and believe everything about their beloved character will be okay. The introspection allows readers to look at what's inside the story player's head while he/she evaluates what's just occurred, the failures, stakes, victories, and how best to proceed in the next scene.

Here are a few tips to slow the story's pace:

☐ Add more description.

- [ ] Choose an active voice using nouns and verbs that have soft consonant sounds.

- [ ] Create longer sentences, paragraphs, and scenes.

- [ ] Detail reaction scenes with character-building introspect.

- [ ] Develop enticing hooks at the beginning and ending of the story in which the urgency is psychological and/or spiritual.

- [ ] Expand dialogue with additional action or internal reflections.

- [ ] Focus on longer words—but not words that send readers to the dictionary.

- [ ] Incorporate figurative speech that uses sensory perception. For example: the crackle of a warm fire, the swirling steam over a hot cup of coffee or tea, sleeping animals, or a peaceful, winding river. A symbol slows the pace by the psychological meaning.

- [ ] Slow the stress and tension.

- [ ] Consider holding back information.

☐ Use more characters in a scene with subplots.

Too many fast-paced action scenes or a continuous, slow-paced narrative ruins a reader's expectations. The writer's goal is to entertain readers with an engaging story.

Story pacing is the writer's means of controlling emotion and mood. Balanced ebb and flow of an unfolding story take the reader to the height of action by controlling the conflict and tension and then ushers in ease only to repeat the process when least expected.

Explore Deeper

1. Take a critical look at your first scene. Are you pleased with the pacing?

2. Does the pacing need to speed up? How do you plan to accomplish this?

3. Does the pacing need to slow down? How do you plan to accomplish this?

4. Explore each scene for pacing, weaving balance and the POV character's goal.

Chapter 10
Writing the Red Herring

Writers value a red herring, a clue designed to deceive the characters and readers. Mystery and suspense writers employ this technique to lead the character and reader to a false conclusion. However, any genre can use it to layer plot if the storyline requires a purposeful misleading of the character(s).

Developing an intriguing red herring is a worthy challenge.

☐ For the writer, developing a red herring takes time and imagination. It's not a simple technique.

☐ For the protagonist, discovering the real culprit requires skill and insight.

☐ For the antagonist, buying time is an opportunity to avoid the truth.

☐ For the reader, absorbing details becomes a challenge of wit and engages interest.

Incorporating a red herring into a plot isn't a series of misunderstandings that label the protagonist as ill-equipped to reach a goal. Instead, the technique adds another level of complexity to an unpredictable story with a maze of evidence. The antagonist is disguised through a carefully crafted plot. As in foreshadowing, the outliner includes the technique in the planning stage while the pantser analyzes the where and when after the first draft. Twist the plot to confuse the protagonist and the reader.

The following ten tips will help the writer successfully create a red herring.

1. The writer incorporates the red herring character into the fabric of the story. The technique isn't an add-on when the plot lacks stress, tension, and conflict.

2. The red herring is an innocent character who has motive to commit a wrongdoing while the real

culprit has nothing established pointing to his/her involvement.

3. The clues aren't easily achieved and are discovered in a deductive manner.

4. The findings are unexpected, and indicators point to the innocent character.

5. The writer establishes an antagonistic setting that works against the red herring. Be selective of where scenes take place. For example: the victim and red herring character undertake dangerous rock-climbing ventures together. The two argue before the climb in front of a witness. One climber falls and meets his death while the red herring character survives. Did the climb cause the fall and subsequent death, or did the surviving character push the victim?

6. The red herring may or may not have a plausible alibi. For example: the character may be afraid and lie about his whereabouts during the time of the crime or request another character to vouch for him. The investigator discovers the ruse, adding more indications of guilt.

7. Sensory perception has the power to persuade. For example: a character detects a distinct smell at the crime and associates the scent with the red herring.

8. The clues prompt other characters and readers to assume the red herring is responsible. The

investigators have worked hard to establish the red herring's guilt.

9. The investigator evaluates statements, evidence, body language, and tangible items near the climax that move the case in a different direction. A character reveals insight regarding the guilty character that others or readers may have overlooked.

10. Stop sign! Don't purposely mislead or deceive the reader. A red herring is believable based on credible evidence.

Red herrings are an essential part of crime and mystery stories, but I encourage you to examine the possibility for any genre. Not every story requires the technique; only the writer can make that decision.

Explore Deeper

1. Does your story's genre routinely employ a red herring?

2. Could your story include a red herring and still follow the guidelines of its genre?

3. Use your imagination and create three ways you could develop a red herring.

4. Write a page in the antagonist's POV in which he/she plans a red herring(s) to mask a crime.

5. Describe your red herring.

6. How will your protagonist learn the false clues have deceived him?

Chapter 11
Developing a Writer's Voice

Developing a writer's voice is not a fill-in-the-blanks exercise. Explanations range from the way a writer pens her prose to how she creates bigger-than-life characters who attract readers with their view on life.

The definition of voice is two-fold:

1. Everything a character experiences, demonstrates, and expresses according to his/her traits.

2. The writer's unique style of writing or author's voice.

Voice shows the writer's fingerprint, a way for readers to identify style. The author's voice is not an intrusion into the story's narrative but a matter of genre, style, word choice, and formatting—the behind-the-scenes workings that show a story through a POV character. The moment an author bypasses the POV character to interject his/her own agenda, the reader senses the storyline has shifted. Something's wrong, even if the reader can't describe it.

A writer's voice isn't birthed overnight. The process takes time—by writing, polishing our craft, and understanding our characters. It's much like our unique conversational style, but with a strong additive: the character's voice. That means no two characters ever quite sound alike. A powerful writing voice doesn't overpower the character but hooks the reader's attention and refuses to let go.

Voice emerges not from studying a textbook, taking a writing course, or reading how-to blog posts and articles, but by how the writer strings words and sentences together. It's a subconscious activity stamped with personal style, word choice, originality, and passion for the project. Our ability to dive into characters and create an adventure strengthens our voice. We weigh each word choice to decide if it's succinct and descriptive.

Donald Maass describes voice: "not only a unique way of putting words together, but a unique sensibility, a distinctive way of looking at the world, an outlook that enriches an author's oeuvre…An original. A standout. A voice."

Voice Considerations

Is the writer using strong verbs and vivid nouns, the ones the characters would use? Has the writer chosen the best word in the character's voice, one the writer is comfortable with?

A writer's genre also influences word choice. A lot to think about, but when a writer tunes out the critics and writes the story of his/her heart with a character they love (or love to hate), the voice emits from their fingertips.

Thomas Merton says about voice: "Not all men are called to be hermits, but all men need enough silence and solitude in their lives to enable the deep inner voice of their own true self to be heard at least occasionally."

I went through several stages of forming my voice while following rules, not following rules, then allowing my writing to morph into my style. When I concentrated on good writing and put the guidelines into perspective, my voice came.

Note: what is appropriate for the genre, style, format, and publisher guidelines is not the same as exploring and finding a unique writer's voice.

The following areas of my voice are important to me. While they may not become part of another writer's voice, they provide an example of the subconscious development that is necessary to establish our writing voice.

☐ I'm a bare-bones writer. I don't like to read paragraphs of description, so I don't write them.

☐ I use humor sparingly and always in character. I can be dark—or I can be flirty. Sometimes a character requires a little more of what I avoid, so I have to weigh my preferences with what the character is telling me—then blend the two. Sometimes all it takes is a single word or phrase to accomplish voice.

☐ I want my personality to show through. Writing doesn't define me, but it is a longing to create a story.

☐ I believe studying genre tone enables a writer to be faithful to the character's perspective with my tone.

☐ I detest exclamation marks. I will stay up all night rewording a scene and dialogue to eliminate that little bat and ball from the end of a sentence. I prefer using word choice, characterization, and the scene's mood to convey emotion. But if an editor believes the placement of an exclamation mark is the best choice, I will present my case … and together we'll decide what works for the sake of the story.

☐ I use only said as a dialogue tag. It's an invisible word and used only to show the speaker. The only other tag I might consider is whisper. I don't use asked as a dialogue tag. The punctuation mark and the syntax show the sentence is a question. Why insult the reader by telling them twice it's an interrogatory sentence?

☐ I want my writing understood immediately. That means not sending readers to the dictionary. Clarity with distinctive nouns and action-packed verbs are more important than the number of syllables in a word.

☐ I don't use semicolons or colons in fiction. In my opinion, a character's actions, thoughts, and dialogue pack more power with one word or a phrased sentence construction.

☐ I refrain from italics for internal dialogue. To me, italics toss the reader out of the adventure.

I emphasize style, word choice, originality, and passion for the project to establish individuality.

☐ I string long and short sentences to create a rhythm and beat designed to keep the reader's interest. However, if an editor deems the use of italics necessary, I'm open for a discussion.

☐ Don't be afraid to be you. A distinct voice means having the confidence to allow your personality to shine through your story.

Outstanding writing comes from composing one sentence after another. That means we write and write to establish our individual style. When a reader says only you could have written that story and they love your way of entertaining them, then you have established your voice.

Explore Deeper

1. How is your writerly voice different from other writers?

2. Genre speaks to a writer's voice. What distinctions mark your genre?

3. Do you write in more than one genre? How does that affect your voice?

4. Do you have certain qualities in your writing that you'd rather not incorporate?

5. Read a page from one of your favorite authors. Now rewrite the page in your voice. What are the differences?

6. List the criteria important to your writer's voice.

Chapter 12
Point of View

The assigned point of view (POV) does matter. The choice presents many challenges—which character, how many, and an opportunity to tell the story from a unique perspective.

Point of view plays a critical role in every story. One character experiences the scene, and that character takes center stage. The character filters every word of the scene through his/her sensory perception and emotions. This allows the writer to pave the way for the reader to live the scene vicariously through the eyes of the character.

To determine the perfect POV, a writer asks the following with the knowledge only one character must surface:

☐ Who has the most to lose?

☐ Why?

☐ What will the character lose if unsuccessful?

☐ What character has the most to gain?

☐ Are the risks/danger/high stakes worth the character's effort?

☐ What role will the character play at the climax?

Most novels are written in either first or third-person and use only one character's viewpoint per scene. This eliminates confusion and keeps the reader engaged. However, if more than one POV is necessary in a scene, use a double space to show the passage continues with a different character. Do this only once per scene.

First Person

Everything is told from the narrator's viewpoint of I or me. The advantage is intimacy. It's easy to believe what the character says, thinks, does, and experiences—like a friend telling you about an event. Or reading someone's diary.

Literary and mainstream novels frequently use first person, but all genres can employ the technique. To the reader, first person often takes on a dual role of character and author, thus increasing emotive conflict right from the beginning. The reader cares.

The disadvantage of first person comes from interjecting the writer's thoughts and feelings instead of using the character's traits. Another challenge is describing the character without the story player sounding self-centered, such as gazing into a mirror or photograph. A third problem is lack of an accurate perspective. The first-person narrator may have unreliable information.

A writer can use a single first-person POV or multiples. If using multiples, identify the viewpoint character's name before the scene or chapter begins.

Second Person

Second person uses you as the point of view character. The story is directed to the reader. Some writers believe this draws the reader deeper into the story and perhaps drive agenda. Other writers view second person as accusatory and drives away readers. This POV appears in short stories but seldom applied to novels. In short, second person can be problematic and not advised for the novice writer.

Third Person

Third person POV is the most prevalent among writers. The author writes about a character, observing what the story player experiences through that character's perspective. The writer uses he, she, it, they, or the character's name.

Multiple third person POVs gives the writer a variety of perspectives to show the story. Be aware that each time a writer changes the POV character, the writer is asking the reader to make a mental adjustment to the new character. Too many changes, and the reader becomes disinterested.

When using multiple points of view, identify the character in the first sentence of each new scene or chapter.

Omniscient

Omniscient point of view means the writer can inhabit several characters' heads at the same time. This perspective makes bonding difficult for the reader to form with a single character. The story may appear distant and confusing, and the reader may not understand why. Omniscient POV leaves little room for the reader to be creative or find a wisp of mystery in the story. Much of classic literature contains the omniscient, but today's reader prefers to be part of the adventure by experiencing a single character, one scene at a time.

Unreliable POV

An unreliable POV uses a biased character who may be lying, mentally or emotionally unstable, or too close to a situation. This viewpoint can be effective in every genre. A character who has an unreliable POV acts and responds with the truth as he/she sees it. As our mind swirls with how we can use this technique, remember if the first person POV character is unreliable all the way through our story, such as in a villain, our reader has to connect with that character early on and his/her motivation.

Deep POV

Deep POV allows the reader to step easily into the viewpoint character's shoes, experiencing every action and reaction through the character's senses. The reader wants to be that character. He/she has stepped into the story player's closet (head) and dressed in those traits and emerged as the POV character.

What appeals to you more: a movie or a 3-D movie event? Deep POV accomplishes the 3-D effect. Agreed, not every scene needs this aspect, so examine your story and characters to see if they're a candidate for a deep point of view.

To master this technique, search for areas in the manuscript where the character sees, hears, tastes, smells, or touches—and rewrite the passage so the character experiences the action. Keywords often signal where the writer has strayed from Deep POV: realized, wondered, scanned, know, recognized, and the sensory tell words: see, hear, taste, smell, and touch. Telling prepositional phrases can also toss the reader out of the character's head.

Deep point of view helps the writer to show rather than tell, but the technique is more about creating a close relationship between the character and reader. The internal dialogue, emotions, and body language must come from the character's heart and mind, providing the reader with more intimacy. Emotions play a huge factor in mastering deep POV, accomplishing two important factors:

1. The reader is more committed to the story because he or she has become the character.

2. The writer takes the mindset "I am the character," instead of "I'm writing about the character."

Rhay Christou: "In deep point of view the character owns the page and the author becomes nonexistent."

Examples

Not Deep POV: I felt the force of the bullet pierce my leg, and I wondered if all the blood was really mine.

Deep POV: A jolt of fiery hot pain seared my leg.

Not Deep POV: She realized he'd been lying to her all along, and the thought brought anger to the surface.

Deep POV: He'd lied to her repeatedly. She slammed her fist onto the table.

How Many Viewpoints?

Writers often ask how many viewpoints are needed to accomplish the theme and purpose of the novel. I've answered this above, but I believe it's worth repeating: every time a writer forces a reader to change a POV, a shift occurs, and a reader must make an adjustment. Choose the minimum number of adjustments necessary to master the story effectively.

How does the setting affect POV? When the choice of POV centers on which character has the most to lose, the setting may be a deciding point, especially if the setting is antagonistic to the protagonist.

Point of View Challenges

Challenges arise in choosing POV when the writer considers unusual character situations. Some of these:

- ☐ Children: Make sure the child's language is accurate. Unique circumstances are the child's cultural, educational, emotional, mental, spiritual, physical attributes and maturity.

☐ A character who is hearing, speech or physically impaired.

☐ A character who has spent his/her life in seclusion.

☐ A character who has never experienced children his/her age.

Varying Degrees

Varying POV degrees set the psychic distance between the reader and the character. According to the goal of the scene and the character's traits and role in the story, a writer can choose first or third person to write distant, close, or intense POV. Powerful scenes emerge from deepening POV to an intense level, but I've also read terrifying scenes from a distant viewpoint. Intense emotional distance calls for deep POV. How far does the writer want to draw the reader into the scene? The distance the writer chooses for the character to internalize what previously occurred varies per:

1. The action prompting the character's reaction.

2. The traits assigned to the character guiding how the character views life in a range of introversion to extraversion.

3. The character's fears and past wounds.

4. The character's goal or problem to solve.

5. The character's knowledge of the incident.

6. The ability of the character to process information honestly.

Some scenes require a close emotional distance, such as a character's revelation or facing a hard truth. Other scenes may have more impact with greater distances, such as a character who doesn't have all the information. An unstable character, especially one who is insensitive, evil or selfish, can set the stage for a gripping scene.

Example

Distant: While having coffee at Starbucks with my neighbor, I glanced out the window. "Look at all the traffic heading into town."

Close: In between sips of coffee at Starbucks with my neighbor, I glanced out the window. "There's one red truck after another heading into town."

Intense: I pointed to the traffic, coughed, and spit hot coffee onto my sweatshirt. "Dad's driving his truck into town. The doctor hasn't released him yet."

Effective POV allows the reader to squeeze herself into every word. The writer chooses what person and the depth according to character and plot.

Explore Deeper

How can you write these with Deep POV?

First-person:
I hurried to my car before the rain soaked me.

First-Person Deep POV:_____
_____
_____
_____

Third Person:
She hurried to her car before the rain soaked her.

Third-Person Deep POV:_____
_____
_____
_____

First-person:

"Please, just one more chance?" I needed this job to survive.

First-Person Deep POV:_____

_____

_____

_____

Third person:

"Please, just one more chance?" She needed the job to survive.

Third-Person Deep POV:_____

_____

_____

_____

With a setting of a bank where a robbery is about to take place, write the scene from the point of view of the character who has the most to lose. You choose and write the scene!

Character A is the robber. He's lost his job and is about to have his home and car repossessed. There's no food in the house, and his wife plans to leave tonight with their two children if he doesn't have the cash to buy groceries.

Character B is an off-duty police officer working a security guard position at the bank. He has a job to do—protect lives and property. His entire life is wrapped up in his career. A month ago, doctors diagnosed him with stage 4 cancer. He's determined to leave his family a heroic legacy.

Character C is the bank teller. The number of errors made lately in her drawer frightens her. In fact, if her drawer doesn't balance soon, she'll lose her job. She's a single mother with two small children and doesn't receive child support.

Character D is a contractor. He has to make a deposit before noon or he'll have several thousand dollars bounce from employees' paychecks. He's an alcoholic and needs a drink badly. He's nervous, irritable, and fearful of losing everything he has. A week ago he learned his only son was killed in a car accident.

Chapter 13
Critical Conflict

Story is about characters in conflict. Without it, the story exists only as an accumulation of sentences. Novelists look at the concept of the story, genre, setting, and all the literary devices to create stress, tension, and conflict. Blend emotions into the mix, especially emotive conflict striving for prominence, and the reader keeps turning pages.

Conflict results from character(s) struggling to achieve wants and needs. The resisting forces (opposition) become a worthy opponent. Desire rules every character's motivation, and the conflict weaves personality and life experiences to form behavior. Combine desires with strengths, values, and flaws, and a complex character emerges who reacts and initiates the conflict in a story. How a character resolves or doesn't resolve conflict reveals who he/she is, the inner person, just as it reveals strengths, weaknesses, and values. I refer to the technique as CC—critical conflict.

Conflict is not a task but a situation to overcome—and an essential component for every successful story. The writer uses the technique to create obstacles in the way of a protagonist or antagonist who is attempting to reach his/her goal. The conflict and character balance the plot; one requires the other to mirror the story world.

Build Conflict Naturally

Throughout this book, I emphasize that character establishes every thought, word, and deed of the storyline. But this also means stress, tension, and conflict result from the inner personality's method of facing conflict.

None of us like to deal with stress, but it has to be in our stories for the reader to experience the point of view character's actions, goals, and emotions. Stress morphs into tension and builds into conflict.

Stress

Stress annoys a character's interpretation of life. If the stress has occurred in the past, the story player uses those lessons to work through the difficulty. If the stress results from a new obstacle, the character searches for new ways to handle the problem. The mentally healthy character has tools to help through stressful moments: a mentor, positive attitude, education, exercise, sound nutrition, proper sleep, relaxation techniques, spiritual aids, and an understanding some situations are out of the character's control.

Tension

The definition of tension is a state in which the muscles are strained tightly. I like the word strained—a tug of war that has the potential to lead to conflict. Tension is more of an antagonistic response and exists between two or more forms of opposition.

One way to increase tension is through dialogue, when the characters speaking are at odds. Marshmallow dialogue accomplishes nothing but wasted word space.

Sol Stein: "Tension produces instantaneous anxiety, and the reader finds it delicious."

Stress and Tension Comparison

Unmanageable stress can push the story player into tension. Although some writers define stress and tension as one category, I'd like to show you the subtle differences.

Stress and tension both apply pressure to a character, but stress is psychological and present before the tension.

Stress escalates to form a challenge, and a character experiences the sensation alone or with others.

A writer establishes tension by continually placing mental, emotional, physical, and/or spiritual barriers in the character's path.

Steven James: "Stories are driven by tension, not events."

Conflict

In everyday life, we normally avoid conflict. It's frustrating, interferes with our plans, and makes life complicated. In a novel, the conflict must captivate and must matter to the reader with high stakes and a significant possibility of failure.

Nancy Kress: "Conflict is the place where character and plot intersect."

Force the reader to grip the steering wheel with the character's emotions: draw them into the thicket or down an icy mountain slope. Shock them. Terrify them. Make them laugh and cry. Give them a time limit, boundaries, and stack up the odds against them. Reward them, then snatch them into another conflict that deems the goal impossible. Draw out every emotion possible.

I first heard this quote from Jerry Jenkins, and a valuable asset to our plotting.

 Jerry Jenkins: "Everything your protagonist does to make things better actually makes things worse."

Inner Conflict

Inner conflict motivates the character into action. For instance, in a romance, a hero's goal may be to win the girl. His outer conflict is he can't ask her out because she has a boyfriend. But his inner conflict may be a terrible fear of rejection because his parents abandoned him when he was young. When the hero overcomes the inner issue, he abates his hindrances to the outer conflict.

Inner conflict must be explosive and powerful. The issues can be mental, emotional, or spiritual, often problems the characters don't want others to see or know. Inner conflict is critical in the black moment or climax.

Strive for every line of a story to have some type of conflict with strong, conflicting emotions. The type of conflict must follow the genre's guidelines, theme, and story premise.

Conflict arises from:

- ☐ Another person
- ☐ Nature
- ☐ Physical
- ☐ Mental
- ☐ Spiritual

Don't put a protective shield around the protagonist. Immerse them into the worst possible situations imaginable—into an abyss that the writer would never venture. Why do we love the Marvel Characters? The writer continuously increases the stakes. Humor adds to the characterization while danger surfaces and provides an exciting story. The writer best achieves this by responding to: what is the worst possible thing that can happen to my character? What is even worse? I challenge you to advance to a third and even fourth level for the ultimate unexpected, unpredictable, and yet believable occurrence.

What creates more conflict?

- [ ] Incorrect understanding of what is going on.

- [ ] The character doesn't have all the information.

- [ ] The character is being lied to or deceived.

- [ ] The character isn't sure he/she is making the right decision.

- [ ] The character is afraid.

Stress, tension, and conflict must always keep the reader glued to the page—and occasionally racing to the medicine cabinet for blood pressure meds.

Explore Deeper

1. On a sheet of paper list your character's temperament, goal, and story problem or goal.

2. List the worst possible scenario that could happen to this character.

3. How does the conflict to the above answer affect your current storyline?

4. Take a breath and develop a scenario that is worse than the one stated in number 2.

5. How does the conflict to the above answer affect your current storyline?

6. Inhale deeply and establish a scenario that is by far worse than number 4.

7. Write the scene based on your last answer.

8. Are you pleased with the results?

Some of your ideas will be discarded while others will help you establish conflict sufficient for building your plot. Do this with your protagonist and antagonist. Use creativity: have the occurrence be the exact opposite of what the reader expects.

Chapter 14
Creating Suspenseful Scenes

Creating a scene, no matter the plotting method, shows an action/reaction or a cause/effect as experienced by a POV character. Writers determine their terminology, but what's important is to show an active progression of the story that subtly displays how the theme moves the protagonist and antagonist ahead in rich tension and conflict to achieve a goal.

The protagonist's goal drives your story. Know it. Memorize it. Breathe it.

Every scene has a POV character stepping onto the page with a goal, conflict, and high stakes. The high stakes don't have to be earth shattering and can be physical or psychological, but the stakes imitate emotion. The opposing focus is the something that must stop the character from achieving his/her goal. This is referred to as scene, action or cause.

The POV character's internal response to what happened previously is called the sequel, reaction or effect. The "catch your breath" portion. Here, the character ponders a dilemma, deliberates what is best to do, and moves forward with a new goal. In these internal responses, the POV character shows the inner character. Unless the character is mentally unstable, he/she will not lie to themselves.

We term novel construction as:

☐ Scene/Sequel

☐ Action/Reaction

☐ Cause/Effect

The key points require a simple equation: every action must have a reaction. In a previous chapter, we explored inner and outer conflict. The reaction portion of each scene is an opportunity for the character to process internally what has previously occurred. Every scene has an inner and outer goal, and the inner occurs before the outer. Sometimes two or three scenes precede the reaction or effect. Keep this area with realistic and unpredictable emotions that show the real inner character.

New writers often make the mistake of overwriting the reaction portion, creating paragraphs of introspect. Today's reader easily grows bored with potential telling. If in doubt, consider what we as readers read. Where do our eyes go? We have a tendency to skip the lengthy paragraph or paragraphs of narrative and set our eyes on the white space—the action—and it's usually dialogue.

While this may sound formulaic, the process shows the writer how to pay due diligence to the craft. Stay on the path … unless a rabbit trail leads the writer to an amazing discovery that enhances the character and plot.

I recommend a four-question technique to pave the way for each scene to maintain consistent breathless action.

1. What is the point of view character's goal or problem to solve?

2. What does the point of view character learn along the way that secures new information?

3. What backstory is revealed? Hold on to the reins of backstory for the first approximately 50 pages. This is where the protagonist is dating the reader, showing he/she is worthy of spending the next 400 pages with. The answers to question 2 and 3 can be identical.

4. How are the stakes raised?

The above four questions allow each scene to have a goal, conflict, and high stakes followed by an internal reaction. Suspense happens in every scene when the reader holds his breath, can't sleep, can't eat, can't function, and can't hold a plausible conversation. The reader fears what could very well happen next because he/she is deeply attached to the protagonist. It's not the fight scenes, the kiss, the actual breakup of a relationship or job that keeps the reader engaged. It's the fear and concern for the character who has captivated the reader to keep turning pages: the rich fullness of believable emotions.

Your mission, if you choose to accept, is to make the impossible occur in such a way that is credible and real. The Marvel movies are a classic example of how incredible comic strip heroes appear realistic by establishing sympathetic characters who have sincere problems which result in incredible conflict. You can't help but like the Marvel characters because they are endearing, sympathetic, and have a problem with a villain. Our characters need the same qualities to move through scene after scene with action that keeps readers on the edge of their seats.

Are you, dear writer, ready to create suspenseful scenes?

Explore Deeper

1. Study the first scene in your book. Answer the four plot questions.

   ☐ What is the point of view character's goal or problem to solve?

   ☐ What does the point of view character learn along the way that is new information?

   ☐ What backstory is revealed?

   ☐ How are the stakes raised?

2. In your first scene, do you see a definite POV character's goal, conflict, and high stakes?

3. Are you successfully condensing the internal reaction of your POV character?

4. How have you woven the inner and outer conflict of this scene?

5. Examine emotions in every scene for realistic reactions.

Chapter 15
Hooking the Reader

We all have our favorite novels, rich stories that transport us into the lives of characters. We walk with them, share their joys and sorrows, weaknesses and strengths, and identify with their problems. But how were we ushered into their lives? By the carefully crafted words of the first line: the hook. Writers spend hours tweaking their first lines and openings.

In ten seconds or less, a reader selects a book from an author, reads the blurb, examines the cover, and turns to chapter one to read the first line. From these first few words, readers decide to continue with the thrill of an adventure or find another book. If they're pleased, they accept the invitation to begin an adventure. Not much time when we consider the hours spent crafting a book and polishing it for publication. The hook establishes the essence of story by creating a curiosity, alarming us, or posing a question—a hint of the conflict to come. It's a subtle promise that every word will be as powerful as the first. My goal is to incorporate the above with an intriguing protagonist who captures the reader from the first word.

No pressure for writers!

Can we demand any less of our writing? None of us want to disappoint our readers. In actuality, the writer may never receive another opportunity to engage the reader into his/her story again.

A writer strives to hook and reel in readers, to entice them to forget about time and lure them into the next approximately 400 pages.

"Come join me in this adventure!"

I like what Donald Newlove says about opening sentences in his book Painted Paragraphs. The imagery and challenge inspire me to create the best possible hook.

Donald Newlove: "It is about the white-hot opening whose glow speaks for a story's greatest strength: its spirit."

So what does the writer need to know before crafting the hook?

1. The genre
2. The characters and their strengths, weaknesses, and goals
3. The theme
4. The plot
5. The writer has set the stage with who, what, where, when, and why.
6. The writer understands the value of sensory perception and setting the stage.

What is incorporated in a good hook?

Every genre needs an alluring first sentence to entice the reader to continue. Study the specifics and the work of the masters to discover what's needed. The hook isn't so much the method of construction as the carefully chosen words used to draw a reader emotionally into the story world.

The following are examples of hooks from both classic and modern literature.

> It is a truth universally acknowledged, that a single man in possession of a good fortune, must be in want of a wife.
>
> ~*Pride and Prejudice* **by Jane Austen**

With the man's first step, the others on the row began a slow tapping on their cell doors.

~Riven **by Jerry Jenkins**

Amos Decker would forever remember all three of their violent deaths in the most paralyzing shade of blue.

~Memory Man **by David Baldacci**

It was the best of times; it was the worst of times ...

~Tale of Two Cities **by Charles Dickens**

"Christmas won't be Christmas without any presents."

~Little Women **by Louisa May Alcott**

Scarlett O'Hara was not beautiful, but men seldom realized it when caught by her charms as the Tarleton twins were.

~Gone with the Wind **by Margaret Mitchell**

Stealing is common here. It's survival.

*~Scattered Link*s **by M. Weidenbenner**

Bad things happened in the dark.

~Lethal Homecoming **by Lynette Eason**

There was a boy called Eustace Clarence Scrubb, and he almost deserved it.

~The Voyage of the Dawn Treader **by C. S. Lewis**

Anything could happen while the dead slept.

~Deep Extraction **by DiAnn Mills**

I had never met a king before.

~The Third Target **by Joel Rosenberg**

Happy families are all alike; every unhappy family is unhappy in its own way.

~Anna Karenina **by Leo Tolstoy**

You better not never tell nobody but God.

~The Color Purple **by Alice Walker**

Opening sentence hooks draw readers into our stories, but end-of-scene and beginning new scene hooks keep readers motivated. Why risk readers closing our book when we can tempt them to continue the thrill? We want readers to lose sleep, ignore dinner preparations, forget to pick up their kids from school, and anything else vying for their attention.

Read your hooks aloud and test them on critique partners. Use sensory perception and a generous portion of mystery. Spend time to perfect every word.

Never give a reader an opportunity to put your book down.

Explore Deeper

1. Reread Donald Newlove's definition of a story's opening in Painted Paragraphs. "It is about the white-hot opening whose glow speaks for a story's greatest strength: its spirit." In your own words, rewrite what this quote means to you.

2. What is your story's spirit?

3. What is your genre? Study the opening lines by your favorite authors.

4. Look at your story's opening line. Does it pose a question, create curiosity, or add an air of mystery? If not, rewrite.

5. Have you ended your scene or chapter with a hook? If not, craft one now.

6. Have you initiated your next scene or chapter with a hook? If not, craft one now.

Chapter 16
Plotting from True Events

Writing a story from an actual person or event provides an opportunity for readers to explore, invoke sensory perception, and imagine themselves as those who lived through a notable time in history. A real or fictitious character who embarks upon the established adventure sets the stage for an incredible story.

The writer borrows information from a source in history or front-page news, but the process has three challenges:

1. How much information can a writer use legally without being guilty of plagiarism?

2. How can the event or person be used to create an intriguing story?

3. If a real person is part of the story and recognized as a hero or heroine, how does the writer show growth and change?

At first glance, the prospect is intriguing. The facts and research are documented and adding characters and fiction to tell the story should be ... easy. But the process requires skill and technique to accomplish the goals of an unforgettable story.

1. A character who steps into a reader's heart and takes permanent residence. He/she is three-dimensional, feeling, thinking, acting and reacting people who have a dynamic backstory that explains behavior in the present.

2. A plot that identifies a problem and employs a complicated means of solving it. Mounting conflict moves the storyline forward.

3. A strong point of view expressed by the character who has the most to lose in any scene. For a recognizable person in history as the protagonist, traits must identify with what is commonly accepted about the person.

4. A credible display of character emotions motivated by the past, present, passion, personality, and persuasion. Life experiences influenced the real person's emotions. Identifying with the person and creating how he/she reacted and responded to various situations can be a tightrope, but when completed effectively, readers will praise the writer.

5. A dialogue linked to genre, culture, setting, and detailed characterization.

6. A setting with strong antagonistic traits.

7. A climax that explodes naturally from all the happenings and events leading up to the black moment.

8. A critical resolution designed to meet reader satisfaction. It must tie all the loose ends and answer all the questions.

The plot doesn't have to match the historical or front-page headlines. Writers take seeds from established facts and massage what's necessary into the character's life. Fascinating backgrounds help writers create a similar or fresh story idea.

The prospect of creating a story from a real person or event is a task worth the hard work.

Explore Deeper

1. What real person or event has inspired you to create a story?

2. Have you established all the documented facts that mirror the figure or event as true?

3. What aspects of the story are challenging?

4. Will the story's climax be something fictitious or previously known?

Chapter 17
The Masterful Beginning

Astory explodes on the first page, and first impressions are lasting. Writers reach deep to please their readers, and let's face it, we writers can't wait to write the story burning inside us.

The beginning is where writers:

1. Show their ability to master characterization with an intriguing point of view character.

2. Introduce a distinct voice.

3. Reveal the conflict to unfold.

4. Create the stage of a powerful and understandable story.

No pressure, writers!

Statistics show a reader decides to purchase a book by the end of the first page. I'm worse! I choose to invest time and energy into reading a book based on the first paragraph, and sometimes the first sentence.

Once writers have established their method of plotting, theme, idea, concept, premise, hook, stress, tension, conflict, setting, and research, they are ready to incorporate these elements into their story beginning.

Before writers place their fingers on the keyboard, they consider what to include on the first page. The beginning highlights the story's genesis.

1. Launch a powerful hook that draws the reader into the story. We established the importance of this aspect in Chapter 15. If a prologue is part of the story, create two opening hooks: one for the prologue, another for Chapter 1.

2. Launch a sympathetic protagonist who endears the reader to the story in the first sentence. Writers need readers to have a glimpse of a story player whom they will care about. We choose how to characterize protagonists and antagonists in a variety of ways that suit our writer's personality. The result is a character with unique traits and authenticity who lives in our readers' hearts long after the story is over.

3. Launch the story's genre: contemporary, historical, romance, suspense, fantasy, science fiction, thriller, western, young adult, or any of the other genres. Pair romance with other genres. The book cover and title often depict the type of story, but it's the writer's responsibility to establish the literary category in the beginning.

4. Launch the story setting. Keep in mind the power of an antagonistic setting that strives to work against the protagonist. Like an antagonistic character, the setting can be charming, attractive, manipulative, and have an emotional impact on the character. See Chapter 5.

5. Launch the basics of a story disturbance with stress, tension, and conflict. While I've repeated these three Musketeers of successful plotting throughout this book, it is essential to a give-me-more type of story. The disturbance isn't the story problem, but a frustrating intrusion into the protagonist's life. Some writers refer to this as the inciting incident. How the character responds creates a bond with the reader who becomes the character's cheerleader. Whatever problems the hero or heroine encounters, the result will be a season of growth and change for the protagonist.

6. Launch the means of showing story date and setting before the text begins.

The first approximately one fifth to one quarter of the novel is the most crucial. The clock is ticking while the reader continues reading or looks for another book. Within these pages a writer labors to form a sympathetic bond between the protagonist and the reader, introduce other characters, and unfold plot—while building conflict and suspense. Too much exposition and readers lose interest. The beginning is not an information dump but a roaring engine of a thrilling ride.

The beginning moves forward with the points from the first page to:

1. Continue strong characterization of the viewpoint protagonist. This story player must come alive, fresh, credible, and with a distinct personality.

2. Continue with fascinating action that leads to increasing suspense. Writers establish these essentials by continuously placing trouble in the protagonist's path.

3. Continue showing the setting in each scene, ensuring it is vital to your plot and antagonistic to the protagonist.

4. Continue with the protagonist's problem to establish the story problem or goal.

After encountering these elements in the beginning of your story, the protagonist accepts the challenge of going after the goal. He/she steps through the first doorway into the plot with a firm resolve to do everything within their power to succeed, including adding to their arsenal of resources.

While moving from scene to scene, the writer increases action with the character's goal, arc, and theme in mind.

In the next chapter, we will look at the sometimes messy, misunderstood middle and show how characters and plot move the story toward a magnificent climax.

Explore Deeper

Examine your first page. Have you incorporated?

1. A strong hook

2. Established genre

3. Introduced a sympathetic character.

4. Set the foundation for a solid bond between the protagonist and the reader.

5. Build the foundation for setting.

Pick one of the four first sentences below and write an opening paragraph that reveals genre and the protagonist.

1. The town's largest population was in the cemetery.

2. The day left no doubt to how many stripes on the American flag.

3. Until this very moment, I thought I was human.

4. The worst of crimes happened on Halloween.

Chapter 18
Managing the Middle

Writers, do you remember as kids we strung a rope across a tree-lined creek or river from one side to the other? We'd line up to grab on tightly and eagerly cross hand over hand, only to find the rope sag in the middle . . . and sometimes break. Our story takes off much like our enthusiasm to reach the other side of the pond without getting drenched. When that happened, we rethought our plan and made changes to ensure success.

Like our attempts to stay dry and reach our destination, our middle can sag and readers are soaked with boring prose. But this won't happen if we carefully plot the scenes and include subplots with unexpected twists and turns.

Rule #1: readers don't care about our stories unless the characters are likable, stakes are high, and the plot is unpredictable.

Consider the character's traits and the story problem. As stated in previous chapters, list the worst unlikely scenarios and a what-if list for all the viewpoint characters. Be over-the-top imaginative. A writer discards some ideas—and uses others to create an intricate storyline. Study the character's psychological traits; there is where the gold mine of issues originate. Our most exciting scenes occur when a character behaves the opposite of what the reader expects. But the reader will accept those actions when the writer has demonstrated the character is not predictable but doesn't exceed personality. Give the readers a moment to take a gasp of air, then drop them back into the action.

Rule #2: the antagonist is an admirable opposing force. Readers value the writer's skill to walk one step ahead of the protagonist.

Elizabeth Sims: "If you could hug the middle of your story, you should be able to feel its bones easily. Your beginning and ending can be fatter and juicier."

A writer can give in to the story dying a slow, cruel death or add plot-additives to keep the reader's attention from the first page to the last.

Ways to avoid the sagging middle

Choices

Reaching the goal is hard work. Our protagonists have doubts, and they make choices in which they must face the consequences of their decisions. Instead of giving your protagonist a right or wrong choice, develop situations that force him/her to choose between two rights or two wrongs. This is one of my favorite techniques.

Complications

New information, unexpected difficulties, eliminate a character, or change the setting.

Crucible

The critical aspect of forming a crucible excels only with high stakes. What can be so powerful, coveted, or needed that the characters involved will not relinquish?

Sol Stein: "A crucible is an environment, emotional or physical, that bonds two people."

Stein continues to say the crucible is a driving point of plot. The environment—either mental or physical bonds two or more people together. The crucible is greater than their desires; neither will give up what matters to them.

Study a few examples of crucibles below:

1. A married couple live an unfulfilled relationship and refuse to divorce because of their children. The children mean more than a loveless marriage.

2. People trapped in an elevator. Who wants to give up the safety?

3. Survivors in a lifeboat. Who will sacrifice his/her life?

4. Soldiers in a war zone. All have to endure danger to save each other.

5. Co-workers who despise each other but must work together on a critical project. The project means more than friction personalities.

Sol Stein: "Remember that the essence of a crucible is that the characters are drawn more to the crucible than escaping from it."

Dialogue

Delete dialogue that merely takes up space or adds to word count.

Gloria Kempton: "Dialogue's purpose, and there is no exception to this, is to creative tension in the present and build suspense for what's to come ... Effective dialogue always, always delivers tension."

Facade

The Cambridge English Dictionary defines facade as, "An outward appearance that is maintained to conceal a less pleasant or creditable reality."

A story facade is a front, show, or pretense that masks what is true or real—until a situation reveals the truth. A protagonist believes something is authentic and projects that to the reader. The reader has no reason to doubt the character. As the story climaxes, the protagonist learns he/she has been deceived. The information proved unreliable, and the protagonist must respond. This brings an unexpected twist to the plot and resolution. Remember the movie Sixth Sense? How long did we watch the story unfold before we "got" it?

Flashbacks

I suggest avoiding flashbacks. This type of story opens in the present and then is written to show how the character got to the point in the beginning. An outstanding example is *The Bridges of Madison County.* This story develops when a brother and sister examine pictures and items from their deceased mother's personal belongings. The more they discover, the more the story unfolds and the viewer, along with the siblings, learn more about their mother's private life than they ever imagined or wanted to know. A phenomenal story and later a movie, but the skill required to accomplish this takes a highly experienced writer.

Opposing Goals

Sol Stein suggests giving characters a different script. The protagonist and antagonist have contrasting agendas. They enter a scene with those goals in mind, not common goals and a struggle ensues.

Secrets

Story secrets add intrigue and emotion to the plot line. The unseen or unknown evokes not only mystery but fear and potential psychological and/or physical danger.

Subplots

Another item to consider in the middle is subplot: Problems involving minor characters who have valid issues or something about a viewpoint character that is separate from the main story idea. Subplots are resolved when the main story problem is concluded.

Toss a wrench

Readers are smart. They consume a story and form opinions, and they believe they know the ending. Many will read to the first doorway, flip pages until the climax, read, and close the book. But if in the middle of the story, a writer tosses a wrench, an event that changes the character and the stakes, then two successful feats are accomplished:

1. No sagging middle but a thrill-packed story.

2. The reader realizes an unpredictable storyline.

The latter portion of the middle is where the climax occurs. This is the total of all the conflict that has spiraled upward since the story's beginning. This is where the reader has no clue how the characters will get out of this mess. A torch ignites the inevitable crisis that has been burning since chapter one. It's catastrophe time. Whatever the protagonist values has been destroyed. Every conceivable emotion must play before the reader through action—spine tingling, heart wrenching action.

The real character—the inner landscape character—must solve the overwhelming problem. And that hero or heroine fulfills all spoken and subtle promises made to the reader.

The middle builds from the moment the protagonist chooses to journey ahead on an adventure. A writer strives to increase the action and suspense to keep the reader engaged. The climax sets the stage for the resolution.

Explore Deeper

1. Evaluate your story's middle. What is your evaluation?

2. What kind of choices have you given your protagonist? Antagonist?

3. Have you developed story complications?

4. Do you have a crucible? Is it needed?

5. Does your story have a facade element? Is it needed?

6. How do you feel about flashbacks?

7. Have you used subplots? How are they connected to the central plot?

8. How did you entice readers to continue reading?

9. How did you change the plot in the middle (wrench)?

Chapter 19
The Anticipated Resolution

The resolution occurs after the climax and shows what happened to the characters after the stress, tension, and conflict were removed at the darkest moment of the story. This last section allows the reader to relax and admire the protagonist's ability to overcome insurmountable odds and achieve success. The protagonist suffered hardships to reach the impossible, and only he or she could have walked the story pages.

Some teachers of fiction refer to the resolution as falling action. However, my thoughts are the resolution is more of character-rewarding time and a display of how the protagonist's struggles were worth the hardships—physical and emotional. The resolution resolves the story problem and adds completeness to the story's strength. Tie up all loose ends with an acceptable conclusion.

The writer crafts a satisfactory ending by not incorporating:

1. Choosing a jolted conclusion with something unexpected on unbelievable.
2. Tossing in new information that alters the course of the story.
3. Surprising the reader with a plot that failed to reach expectations.
4. Ignoring reader promises.
5. Forgetting to tie up all loose ends, including any subplots introduced.
6. Forgetting genre guidelines.

None of the above are wise ways to conclude a story because the writer has betrayed the reader's confidence. Frustration invades the reader because he/she signed on for an adventure and the story ending punched with disappointment.

Writers end the story naturally by showing how the protagonist struggled to change a happening or event in an admirable way. A story ending that concludes the protagonist's quest satisfactorily confirms the reader's next book will be by the writer who provided the adventure.

Explore Deeper

1. Has your character changed throughout the story? How?

2. According to the story's genre, what must occur at the conclusion?

3. According to the story's genre, what do you need to re-examine?

4. As the writer, how have you changed as a result of creating the story? Describe.

5. What weaknesses have you discovered in your plot? How will you strengthen those areas?

Chapter 20
Final Thoughts

Writers search for clever means to the raise the stakes for the protagonist. We dig deep within the character's landscape to make the protagonist squirm and force him/her to manage challenges by relying on his/her strengths and growing the protagonist into a genuine hero or heroine. The extra work eliminates many story pitfalls.

E.A. Bucchianeri: "If typos are God's way of keeping a writer humble, plot holes certainly keep one on their knees."

Writers often turn to obvious means of adding stress, tension, and conflict through plot twists, setting, dialogue, emotive conflict, symbolism, characterization, and other literary techniques. Those are powerful tools, and writers explore their use to create an exciting plot line.

Previously in Chapter 18, we discussed how to avoid the sagging middle. A review of that chapter shows how to increase stakes by building tension and conflict throughout every scene.

To ensure tight, high-stakes scenes, use the character's fears and weaknesses against him/her. This causes the character to not only struggle but also to face an inner and outer antagonist: fear and setting. A review of Chapter 7 regarding fear should assist. Watch plot twists emerge that will add levels to the story line. Seek ways to ensure the character faces one difficult situation after another.

Tips to increase the stakes:

1. Create a time element or ticking clock to prevent the protagonist's worst possible scenario from a successful resolution.

2. Add complications that apply pressure to the hero/heroine. Use other characters, backstory, betrayal, internal turmoil, blind spots, and circumstances beyond the protagonist's control.

3. Force the protagonist to make tough choices and be willing to accept the consequences. For example, two rights or two wrongs as described in Chapter 18.

4. Give the antagonist an edge that deems the protagonist's goal impossible. Create a synopsis in the antagonist's POV in which he reaches his/her goal. Use those barriers to heighten the suspense and worry the reader about the protagonist's ability to succeed.

5. Punch the story with unpredictable and unexpected events.

6. Implore credibility by showing characters in action with powerful motivation, even wrong ones.

7. Develop an antagonistic setting for every scene.

8. Keep any type of relief at a distance until the climax and resolution.

Angus Fletcher: "Create a story world with a deep problem that the world or the character refuses to acknowledge."

Checklist for plot construction

1. Opens directly with the POV character's problem or goal.

2. The scene stays in the POV character's head.

3. There is a distinct reason for the scene.

5. The scene follows the four plot questions.

6. The scenes capture an antagonistic setting.

7. The scene uses dialogue that is in character and in conflict with another character. It has energy, excitement, stress, tension, and builds conflict.

8. The scene uses narrative sparingly.

9. The scene shows what is happening in fresh, unique, unexpected, and believable action.

10. The scene uses inner and outer conflict.

11. The scene ends with the highest possible stakes.

12. According to the writer's method of constructing a story, create a spreadsheet that shows the POV character, the scene goal, and outcome.

Exploring the art of plotting is an adventure in character. The more a writer knows about a character, the more the story line will resonate with the reader.

I conclude with a favorite quote from Donald Maass.

Donald Maass: "A work of fiction grips our imaginations because we care, both about the characters in the tale and about ourselves. To put another way, we are concerned about the outcome of the story because what is happening to the characters could happen to us."

May your story entertain, inspire, and encourage readers with a thrilling adventure.

Explore Deeper

1. How have you increased the stakes in your story?

2. Are you pleased with the level of stress, tension, and conflict throughout each scene?

3. Have you applied the checklist for plot construction in your story?

4. What is your story missing?

5. Are you ready to plot your story?

Recommended Writing Books List

The Emotion Thesaurus – Angela Ackerman & Becca Puglisi

The Emotional Wound Thesaurus – Angela Ackerman & Becca Puglisi

Conflict and Suspense – James Scott Bell

Fiction Attack! – James Scott Bell

Plot and Structure – James Scott Bell

The Five Love Languages – Gary Chapman

The Art of Character – David Corbett

Wired for Story – Lisa Chron

Goal, Motivation, and Conflict – Debra Dixon

On Becoming a Novelist – John Gardner

I know What You are Thinking – Dr. Lillian Glass, Ph.D

Dialogue – Gloria Kempton

On Writing – Stephen King

Characters, Emotion & Viewpoint – Nancy Kress

Story Trumps Structure – Steven James

Troubleshooting Your Novel – Steven James

The 12 Pillars of Novel Construction – C.S. Lakin

The Emotional Craft of Fiction – Donald Maass

The Fire in Fiction – Donald Maass

Writing the Breakout Novel – Donald Maass

Writing the Breakout Novel Workbook – Donald Maass

Writing 21st Century Fiction – Donald Maass

Word Painting – Rebecca McClanahan

Story – Robert McKee

Exploring the Art of Character – DiAnn Mills

The Power of Body Language – Tonya Reiman

How to Grow a Novel – Sol Stein

Stein on Writing – Sol Stein

Creating Character Arcs – K.M. Weiland

The Moral Premise – Stanley D. Williams

Meet DiAnn

DiAnn Mills is a bestselling author who believes her readers should expect an adventure. She weaves memorable characters with unpredictable plots to create action-packed, suspense-filled novels. DiAnn believes every breath of life is someone's story, so why not capture those moments and create a thrilling adventure?

Her titles have appeared on the CBA and ECPA bestseller lists; won two Christy Awards, the Golden Scroll, Inspirational Readers' Choice, and Carol award contests.

DiAnn is a founding board member of the American Christian Fiction Writers, a member of Advanced Writers and Speakers Association, Mystery Writers of America, the Jerry Jenkins Writers Guild, Sisters in Crime, and International Thriller Writers. She is the director of the Blue Ridge Mountains Christian Writers Conference and Mountainside Retreats: Marketing, Nonfiction, Novelists, and Speakers with social media specialist Edie Melson. DiAnn continues her passion of helping other writers be successful. She speaks to various groups and teaches writing workshops around the country.

DiAnn has been termed a coffee snob and roasts her own coffee beans. She's an avid reader, loves to cook, and believes her grandchildren are the smartest kids in the universe. She and her husband live in sunny Houston, Texas.

DiAnn is very active online and would love to connect with readers on: Facebook, Twitter, Instagram, Pinterest, Goodreads, BookBub, YouTube, LinkedIn MeWe, or her website: diannmills.com

Made in the USA
Middletown, DE
04 October 2022

11950099R00097